Ultimate Travel Guide To

Cork, IRELAND

Discover the Magic of Cork: Your Passport to Unforgettable Adventures

Elizabeth Whyte

COPYRIGHT NOTICE

DISCLAIMER

Please note that the information contained within this document is for educational purposes only. The information contained herein has been obtained from sources believed to be reliable at the time of publication. The opinions expressed herein are subject to change without notice.

Readers acknowledge that the Author / Publisher is not engaging in rendering legal, financial or professional advice. The Publisher / Author disclaims all warranties as to the accuracy, completeness, or adequacy of such information.

The Publisher assumes no liability for errors, omissions, or inadequacies in the information contained herein or from the interpretations thereof. The publisher / Author specifically disclaims any liability from the use or application of the information contained herein or from the interpretations thereof.

TABLE OF CONTENT

Table of Contents

Introduction

INTRODUCTION TO CORK, IRELAND!

Hello, fellow traveler! Buckle up, because I'm about to take you on a tour of Cork, Ireland's fascinating city. I'm excited to share my experiences and insights with you after having lately discovered this hidden gem.

Overview of Cork

Cork, sometimes known as the "Rebel City," is located on Ireland's southern coast and emits a distinct charm that is difficult to describe. Consider beautiful mansions surrounding the Lee River, lively marketplaces, and a vibe that is both historic and modern.

Despite being Ireland's second-largest city, it maintains a welcoming, small-town character. It's like walking through a patchwork quilt of distinct neighborhoods, each with their own personality and narrative to tell.

Cork's Rich History

You can feel the echoes of centuries past as you walk along the cobblestone streets. Cork's history is as compelling as its natural beauty. Every corner appears to whisper stories of resilience and revolt, from Viking settlers to medieval periods and up to the struggles for Irish independence.

Visit Cork City Gaol, a historic jail turned museum where you may put yourself in the shoes of nineteenth-century prisoners. The stories of historical individuals like Michael Collins enrich Cork's narrative in a way that is both educative and touching.

Cork's Geographical Features

Cork's diversified terrain was one of the first things that impressed me. The River Lee winds its way through the city, producing a complex network of waterways. You'll come across gorgeous bridges and come across picturesque sites like Fitzgerald Park, ideal for a leisurely afternoon stroll.

A little further on, you'll come across the rocky beauty of County Cork. The Wild Atlantic Way entices with its towering cliffs, rolling hills, and breathtaking coastal views. Cork's landscape has something for everyone, whether you enjoy hiking, driving, or simply taking in the beauty.

Why Visit Cork?

"Why should Cork be my next travel destination?" you may be wondering. The answer, my friend, is as varied as the city itself.

- **Cultural Fusion:** Cork's rich past merges harmoniously with its dynamic current culture. Traditional Irish music may be heard in bars and cutting-edge art galleries, creating a beautiful blend that caters to all interests.

- **Culinary Delights:** Get ready for a culinary experience. Cork is a foodie's paradise, with the famed English Market providing a sensory overload. Fresh local fruit, excellent cheeses, and delectable pastries abound in Cork's culinary scene.

- **Warm Hospitality:** The people of Cork are noted for their friendliness and kindness. Don't be shocked if you end yourself having interesting talks with the locals at the pub. Their sincere warmth provides a special touch to your Cork experience.

- **Gateway to the Wild Atlantic Way:** Cork is an excellent starting point for exploring the Wild Atlantic Way if you are a wildlife enthusiast. The rough coastline, beautiful villages, and breathtaking scenery combine to create an amazing road trip.

Chapter 1

GETTING READY FOR YOUR TRIP

Let's make sure you're ready for an incredible journey before we dive into the enchantment of Cork. After spending some time navigating the ins and outs of this Irish wonderland, here are some pointers to make your trip to Cork as smooth as a pint of Guinness.

Travel Planning

- **Why choose Cork?**

First and foremost, why Cork? Imagine a metropolis that seamlessly integrates historic past with a lively present, surrounded by County Cork's stunning scenery. Cork has something for everyone, whether you're a history buff, a foodie, or an outdoor enthusiast.

- **Making a Budget**

Let's talk about money. Cork isn't the most affordable destination in Europe, but don't worry, fellow tourists. You can enjoy everything Cork has to offer without breaking the budget if you plan ahead of time. When planning your budget, keep in mind the costs of lodging, daily meals, transportation, and activities. Don't forget to make room for a few keepsakes!

- **Best Time to Visit Cork**

Ah, the eternal travel question: when's the best time to go? My recommendation? Aim for the months of May through September. The weather is pleasant, and you'll be able to see the city in full flower. However, if you're looking for some Irish mist and reduced pricing, the off-season might be just as appealing.

- **Passport and Visa Information**

Let's get the details out of the way first. Check the expiration date on your passport and ensure it will be your faithful companion throughout your Cork adventure. Fortunately for most of us, Ireland is a member of the European Union, which means no visa is necessary for EU nationals. Non-EU visitors should check the visa requirements well in advance.

- **Travel Insurance**

I cannot emphasize this enough: do not scrimp on travel insurance. Cork is all about adventure, and you want to be prepared for any unforeseen turns. A solid travel insurance policy is your safety net for everything from medical crises to misplaced bags. Trust me, you'll be grateful for the peace of mind when you're touring Cork City's tight lanes.

Accommodation

Cork's Accommodation Kaleidoscope

Now that the details have been worked out, let's talk about where you can lay your tired head. Cork has a wide range of lodging alternatives to suit all preferences and budgets. There's something for everyone, from lovely bed and breakfasts to sophisticated hotels and cozy vacation homes.

- **Hotels**

If you enjoy the rush and bustle of city life, living in Cork City's core is your best bet. There are a variety of hotels to suit all budgets. The River Lee Hotel, for example, provides not only a nice accommodation but also spectacular views of the River Lee.

- **Bed & Breakfast**

Consider a bed and breakfast for a more intimate encounter. You'll get a personal flavor of Irish hospitality, with hosts eager to share local advice and anecdotes. Garnish House, for example, provides a pleasant feel while being ideally positioned for experiencing the city.

- **Vacation Rentals**

Vacation rentals could be your golden ticket if you're traveling with a group or staying for a prolonged period of time. Platforms like Airbnb provide a wealth of possibilities for making you feel perfectly at home in Cork, from quaint cottages in the countryside to sophisticated apartments in the city center.

Transportation

Getting to Cork

How can you travel to this Irish paradise? Cork is well-connected by air, with aircraft from major European cities arriving at Cork Airport. If you're driving down from Dublin, you can take a lovely rail ride or brave the

Irish roads. The voyage to Cork, regardless of means of transportation, is a prelude to the wonders that await.

- **Public Transportation**

Getting around Cork is simple once you've arrived. The city boasts a well-functioning public transit system that includes buses and trains. If you want to go exploring in the outskirts, consider renting a car. Simply be prepared to enjoy the thrill of driving on the left side of the road!

- **Cycling in Cork**

Cycling in Cork is an incredible treat for the environmentally aware and the daring. Cycling is encouraged in the city and its surroundings, with designated lanes and attractive routes. You can rent bikes from numerous locations across the city, and trust me when I say that discovering Cork on two wheels adds a whole new depth to your journey.

Packing Tips

- **Weather, Layers, and More**

Let's talk about packing, which is an art form in and of itself. Cork's weather can be as varied as its surroundings. Layers are your best friend, along with waterproofs for the inevitable Irish drizzle. Remember to bring sturdy walking shoes for city explorations and country walks. And, of course, a universal travel adaptor, because no one wants to be stuck in the midst of Blarney Castle with a dead camera or phone.

- **Important Items**

Aside from the obvious suspects - passports, tickets, and so on - there are a few Cork-specific must-haves. A reusable water bottle (to stay hydrated on lengthy treks), a daypack for your adventures, and a power bank to keep your electronics charged so you can capture every wonderful moment.

- **What not to Bring**

Leave the heavier winter clothing at home; Cork rarely gets below freezing. Also, unless you're going to one of Cork's finest eating venues, skip the formal attire. Keep things casual and comfy - after all, you're in Ireland!

Now that you've gathered your supplies, it's time to plunge into the heart of Cork. Prepare for a tour full of history, fun, and possibly a pint or two along the way. Sláinte!

Chapter 2

ACCOMMODATION

Now that we've sorted out the logistics, let's get into one of the most fun elements of trip planning: locating an ideal place to stay during your Cork vacation. I know we talked a little bit about it in chapter 1, but this is so important that it warrants some more attention.

After wandering around the cobblestone lanes and snug corners, here are my thoughts on the many accommodation options available in this Irish gem.

Hotels

Cork's Hotel Scene

Let's start with hotels: Cork has a wide range of options to suit every budget, from opulent getaways to budget-friendly havens. The River Lee Hotel, located right on the water, is a gem. The accommodations have beautiful views of the Lee River, and the location is convenient to the city's busy center. It's the ideal combination of modern luxury with Irish charm.

The Imperial Hotel is ideal for visitors looking for a historic flair. This iconic restaurant, which dates back to 1813, oozes old-world elegance. The hotel's nicely designed rooms and central location make it an ideal starting point for exploring Cork City on foot.

Bed and Breakfasts

Embracing Irish Hospitality

Cork's bed & breakfasts are the way to go if you want a more intimate and personal experience. I had the pleasure of staying at Garnish House, a wonderful bed and breakfast maintained by friendly hosts. It's a calm sanctuary in the center of the city, with a garden that feels like a hidden oasis. The personalized touches and substantial Irish breakfast set the tone for each day of adventure.

The Gabriel House, located on the outskirts of the city center, is another hidden gem. The Victorian-era structure has been painstakingly renovated, and the cozy rooms are furnished in period style. What I appreciated the most were the hosts' insider insights and recommendations - it felt like I was staying with friends who knew all of Cork's hidden gems.

Vacation Rentals

Living Like a Local

Vacation homes in Cork are plenty for people seeking the comforts of home and a little more independence. During my trip, I chose a nice Airbnb accommodation. The comfort of having my own kitchen for slow mornings and the sense of fitting in with the locals enhanced my Cork experience.

Consider a nice home on the outskirts if you're traveling in a group. Drombeg Stone Circle Cottage, a lovely getaway near Glandore, caught my eye. Surrounded by nature and historical monuments, it's an ideal getaway for anyone looking for peace and quiet while still being close to Cork City.

Choosing the Right Accommodation

Consider the ambiance you want when choosing your accommodations. If you want to be in the middle of the activity, a hotel or central B&B may be your best bet. A vacation rental or a B&B in a quieter neighborhood may be the way to go if you prefer a more relaxed atmosphere and the opportunity to live like a local.

Pro Tip: Always read reviews and contact hosts or hotel personnel if you have any questions. A personal touch can make all the difference in ensuring your lodging matches your travel style.

Cork's Accommodation Kaleidoscope

What impressed me the most about Cork's accommodation scene was its rainbow of options. Cork has something for everyone, whether you're a solitary traveler searching for a cozy corner, a couple looking for a romantic hideaway, or a family looking for a home away from home.

As you settle into your chosen lodging, you're not just securing a place to sleep; you're immersing yourself in Cork's distinct personality. Each option adds a particular flavor to your Cork journey, whether it's the history oozing through the walls of a centuries-old hotel, the warm hospitality of a B&B, or the independence of your own vacation rental.

So, as you go on your Cork adventure, make your choice of lodging more than just a place to sleep, but a vital part of the voyage. Sláinte to the warm greetings, cozy beds, and memories waiting to be formed in the heart of Ireland!

Chapter 3

TRANSPORTATION

Now that we've discovered our gorgeous Cork accommodations, let's talk about how to explore this fascinating city and its surroundings. Cork has a variety of transportation alternatives for any type of traveler, from planes to bicycles.

Getting to Cork

Flying into the Emerald Isle

Getting to Cork is simple, especially if you fly. Cork Airport, Ireland's southern gateway, greets you with that particular Irish charm. My journey began with a flight, and as I touched there, the excitement of discovering Cork's cobblestone streets and colorful atmosphere grew.

Cork Airport is a short taxi or bus ride from the city center, so you can begin your adventure almost immediately after landing. If you're coming from Dublin, consider taking the train for a lovely ride through the picturesque Irish countryside.

Public Transportation

City Buses and Beyond

Cork has an excellent public transportation system that makes it easy to get around the city and its surroundings. Buses are the preferred means of transportation for visiting the city core, and the network includes nearly every nook and hole. The double-decker buses provide not just transit but also a moving vantage point, providing panoramic vistas as you navigate the mountainous streets.

Train Journeys Throughout History

The train system is a hidden gem for day getaways or exploring farther into the Irish landscape. The beautiful architecture of Cork Kent train station serves as the starting point for scenic travels. I boarded a train to Cobh, a seaside town steeped in naval heritage. The train's regular clatter provided a nostalgic soundtrack to the voyage, making me feel as if I were journeying back in time.

Car Rentals: Freedom on Irish Roads

Driving into the countryside

Renting a car gives you the maximum flexibility to explore at your own speed. Cork's roads are a pleasure to drive, weaving through emerald-green scenery and along scenic seaside paths. I chose a rental car to explore the countryside, and it was one of the best decisions I had made.

I marveled at the craggy cliffs and pristine beaches as I cruised down the Wild Atlantic Way, stopping whenever a magnificent scene demanded my attention. Having your own set of wheels transforms your Cork trip into a customized journey, whether it's the Ring of Kerry, the Cliffs of Moher, or the delightful villages along the road.

Driving Tips in Ireland

Driving in a new nation might be scary, especially if you're used to driving on the opposite side of the road, as I am. Not to worry! Irish drivers are courteous, and the roads are well-kept. Take your time, accept the occasional roundabout snarl, and revel in the freedom of the wide road.

Cycling in Cork: Two-Wheeled Bliss

- **Pedaling Through the City and Countryside**

Cycling in Cork is an incredible delight for the environmentally conscious and those who enjoy active discovery. The city is bike-friendly, with designated bike lanes winding through the streets and along the Lee River. I decided to indulge in two-wheeled ecstasy by renting a bike for the day.

I felt like a local while cycling down the riverbanks, passing by students, families, and even other tourists on their own bicycling experiences. The pace was ideal for soaking in the city's beauty, and with the wind in my hair, I discovered hidden jewels like Fitzgerald Park and the Cork City Gaol.

- **Cycling Routes beyond the City**

The cycling culture extends beyond the city limits, with various routes available for those wanting a rural escape. The Great Southern Trail, an abandoned railway route that has been converted into a cycling path, is ideal for a day excursion.

I cycled through lush forests, charming villages, and even discovered a small farmers' market - a full immersion into rural Irish life.

Choosing Your Mode of Transportation: A Personal Preference

Choosing the best means of transportation in Cork is determined by your travel preferences. If you're in the city center and want to take in the atmosphere, public transit is both quick and affordable. A rental car opens the full possibilities of your experience for day trips and visiting the surrounding area.

Cycling may be the right option for you if, like me, you enjoy the sense of the wind in your hair and the freedom of the open road. Whatever method of transportation you pick in Cork, it contributes its own distinct flavor to your journey.

Final Thoughts

When I think back on my stay in Cork, I'm grateful for the various modes of transportation that allowed me to explore the city's charming streets and the breadth of County Cork.

Cork's transportation tapestry is a vital part of the trip, whether it's the excitement of driving along seaside cliffs, the rhythmic hum of a train journey, or the simple joy of biking through the city.

So, while you plan your Cork adventure, think about the type of voyage you want to have.

Whether it's the ease of buses, the independence of your own car, or the eco-friendly allure of cycling, each method of transportation becomes a character in your Cork journey.

Sláinte to the roads, trains, and rivers - may they lead you to the heart of the Emerald Isle!

Chapter 4

PACKING TIPS

Let's dig into the art of packing now that we're knee-deep in the thrill of organizing your Cork adventure. Cork, with its changeable weather and numerous activities, necessitates a deliberate approach to what you pack. So select your favorite travel bag and join us as we unravel the mysteries of smart packing!

Weather Considerations

Cork's Weather Waltz

Packing for Cork is like to getting ready for a fanciful dance with the elements. The weather here is like a multifaceted gem: it can glitter with sunlight, sway with delicate mist, or surprise you with a downpour. What is the key? My fellow passengers, layers, layers.

I went in the summer, and let me tell you, it's not all rainbows and sunshine. There are, in fact, rainbows - plenty of them. Cork's weather is unpredictable, so packing a variety of t-shirts, sweaters, a waterproof jacket, and a strong umbrella is a good idea. I can't tell you how many times I've seen the sun burst through the clouds, generating those amazing rainbow moments.

Footwear for the Cobbled Ballet

Cork's streets are a delightful cobblestone dance - nice to look at but potentially dangerous if you're wearing the incorrect shoes. Your best buddies are comfortable, waterproof shoes. You'll want to be quick as you tour the steep city and its surroundings.

Essential Items: The Cork Survival Kit

- **Reusable Water Bottle: Stay Hydrated on the Go**

Let's start with the necessities - the little things that can make or break your Cork vacation. A reusable water container is essential first and foremost. Staying hydrated is essential either exploring the city or hiking in the countryside. It's also eco-friendly, and Cork, with its emphasis on sustainability, would approve.

- **Daypack: Your Dependable Travel Companion**

Purchase a nice daypack. A trustworthy daypack is your trusty buddy whether you're cycling along the River Lee, strolling through the English Market, or hiking in County Cork. It'll hold your essentials, free up your hands for taking shots, and, of course, serve as a home for any souvenirs you may pick up along the trip.

- **Power Bank: Keep the Memories Alive**

Cork is a town you'll want to remember for its dynamic city life, magnificent surroundings, and unexpected joy. A power bank is a must-have travel item to ensure that your camera and phone don't die in the middle of a perfect image. Nothing is more frustrating than missing a postcard-worthy moment because your phone decided it needed a snooze.

- **Adapters: Stay Connected Worldwide**

The dance of the adapters, eh? Cork, like the rest of Ireland, utilizes the Type G plug. Pack the necessary adapters to keep your gadgets charged and ready to go. You wouldn't want to miss out on uploading those envious images from your Cork vacation, would you?

What Not to Bring: Lightening the Load for Maximum Enjoyment

- **Heavy Winter Gear: Leave the Parka at Home**

Heavy winter gear is one item you can leave behind. Even in the winter, Cork rarely gets freezing temperatures. Instead, concentrate on layers that can adapt to changing weather. A warm sweater and a waterproof jacket will be more useful than a heavy parka.

- **Formal Wear: Embrace Casual Comfort**

Unless you're going to one of Cork's finest restaurants, skip the formal attire. The city's mood is relaxed and laid-back, and you'll feel more at ease blending in with the locals if you dress casually and comfortably.

- **Excessive Electronics: Immerse Yourself in the Moment**

While having your camera and phone is necessary, avoid going overboard with gadgets. Cork's allure is found in its streets, people, and surroundings. Allow yourself to be fully present in the moment by taking a vacation from the continual digital noise.

When you're enjoying a tranquil moment by the River Lee or the boisterous atmosphere at a classic Irish pub, you'll thank yourself.

The Art of Packing: A Personalized Canvas

Remember that packing is an art, not a science as you stand in front of your open luggage. It's about building a canvas that improves rather than hinders your vacation experience. Cork, with its unique mix of urban activity and natural beauty, need an adaptable wardrobe as well as a few travel-friendly pieces.

Consider the weather as a dancing partner, be prepared for unexpected moments, and leave anything that may weigh you down behind. Consider the adventures that await you as you pack for Cork: cobblestone streets, rolling hills, cozy pubs, and the warmth of Irish friendliness. Your suitcase is more than simply a place to store your belongings; it's a gateway to the heart of the Emerald Isle.

So, as you pack your bag and set out on your Cork journey, pack with intention, leave room for spontaneity, and prepare to unravel the intricacies of this wonderful Irish city.

Sláinte to the art of packing, the pleasure of discovery, and the memories waiting to be built in Cork's heart!

Chapter 5

EXPLORING CORK CITY

Let me be your guide through the vivid tapestry of Cork City as we tie up our walking shoes and prepare to meander over the cobblestone streets. This chapter is a tour into the essence of this enchanting Irish treasure, from the vibrant St. Patrick's Street to the culinary utopia of The English Market and the melancholy history of Cork City Gaol.

Cork City Center: Where Every Corner Tells a Story

Cork's Distinct Vibe

The recognizable aura of Cork greets you as you enter the city center - a wonderful blend of historic charm and contemporary excitement. The city's compact size makes it ideal for walking, and every corner seems to whisper stories from a bygone era.

St. Patrick's Street: A Shopper's Paradise and More

Strolling down the thoroughfare

Let's start our journey on St. Patrick's Street, the bustling thoroughfare that acts as Cork's business and cultural center. With a mix of high-street brands, boutique shops, and traditional Irish establishments, this busy strip is a shopaholic's dream.

I was captivated by the vivid energy as I wandered down St. Patrick's Street. Every step seemed like a celebration of Cork's vitality, with musicians playing on street corners, the aroma of fresh flowers from market booths, and the lively talk of people. Make time for leisurely window shopping and possibly picking up a few unique items.

The Architectural Symphony

The architectural symphony of antique buildings with colorful facades standing shoulder to shoulder with new constructions was one of the things that drew my eye on St. Patrick's Street. It's like going on a time machine, with each structure narrating a different tale of Cork's history. Don't forget to glance up; the elaborate embellishments on the façade are a monument to yesteryear's craftsmanship.

The English Market: A Culinary Odyssey in Cork

An Eclectic Culinary Haven

As we enter The English Market, let's switch from shopping bags to food bags. This historic market, which has been in operation since 1788, is a gastronomic wonderland that draws foodies from all over the world. As you enter this gourmet paradise, prepare your taste senses for a symphony of tastes.

The vivid colors of fresh produce, the rich perfume of artisanal cheeses, and the sizzle of street food kiosks making exquisite sweets met me as I walked through the market. Local sellers offer their stories and recommendations enthusiastically, bringing a personal touch to the gastronomic journey.

Must-Try Delights

The English Market is more than simply a location to buy ingredients; it's also a place to sample the best of Irish cuisine. At the Farmgate Café, where locally sourced foods are transformed into culinary masterpieces, indulge in a classic Irish breakfast. Don't forget to bring some fresh seafood or exquisite pastries for a relaxing picnic by the Lee River.

Cork City Gaol: A Look Back at Ireland's Past

From Prison to Museum

A visit to the Cork City Gaol is a must as we explore further into Cork's history. This enormous structure, which is now a museum, provides a harrowing view into Ireland's prison history. The self-guided tour takes you through the haunting chambers, illustrating the horrific conditions that prisoners experienced in the nineteenth century.

The panoramic view of the city from the top of the Gaol tower is both breathtaking and haunting. It serves as a vivid reminder of the sufferings and fortitude of individuals who were previously confined within these walls. The Cork City Gaol is more than a museum; it's a voyage back in time that has a lasting impression.

Historical Landmarks: Traveling Through Cork's Rich Past

Let's dust off our time machines and go around Cork's historical sites, where every brick tells a story and every cobblestone echoes with the whispers of centuries past.

Cork City Hall: A Grandeur of Architecture and Heritage

The Architectural Wonder

Cork City Hall, which stands magnificently along the River Lee, is a testimony to the architectural magnificence of Cork. The magnificent façade, embellished with elaborate carvings and imposing columns, quickly drew my attention as I approached. This landmark structure, built in the French Renaissance style, combines historical grandeur with a modern twist.

Enter the World of History

Upon entering, I was surrounded by echoes of Cork's history. The inside is a museum in and of itself, with exhibitions highlighting the city's rich history and cultural legacy. The journey inside Cork City Hall is like flipping through the pages of a live history book, with interactive exhibitions and interesting relics.

Shandon Bells and Tower: A Musical Journey Through Time

Through the Ages of Ringing

A short walk from the city center brought me to the Shandon Bells & Tower, one of Cork's most iconic sights. The distant tinkling of bells began to accompany my journey as I approached the tiny stairway of St. Anne's Church. With each stride, I got closer to the center of this musical paradise.

Panoramic Pinnacle Views

When I got to the top, I was greeted with panoramic views of Cork and beyond. The River Lee snaked across the terrain, and the brilliant colors of the houses presented a picture of a city rich in history. The Shandon Bells, with their sweet tones, are not only a musical treat for the ears, but also a reminder of Cork's resilient character.

Elizabeth Fort: A Fortress in Time

Cork's Sentinel Over the Centuries

I went a little further and discovered Elizabeth Fort, a powerful fortification that has stood guard over Cork since the 17th century. I couldn't help but envision the decades of stories engraved in the gigantic stone walls as I approached them.

Views Fit for Royalty

Climbing to the fort's summit provided me with amazing views over Cork City. The vast countryside, set against the historic stone walls, provided a visual feast. Elizabeth Fort not only provides a peek into Cork's military history, but it also serves as a vantage point connecting the city's past and lively present.

Green Retreats: Parks and Gardens

Embracing Nature in the Urban Jungle

Let us now take a break from the historical immersion and explore the green getaways that beautify Cork. Parks and gardens, with their serenity and natural beauty, give a welcome respite from the city's hectic streets.

Fitzgerald Park: A Riverside Retreat

Floral Symphony by the Lee

Fitzgerald Park, tucked along the banks of the Lee River, is a tranquil haven for tired travelers. The vivid colors of the flower beds and the sweet aroma of blooming roses created a sensory symphony as I strolled through the park. The antique monuments, especially the famed Berwick Fountain, complemented the natural canvas with artistic elegance.

Lazy afternoons and leisurely strolls

The park is great for leisurely strolls, picnics, or simply relaxing in the heat of a bright afternoon. The sweeping green lawns invite both locals and visitors to relax, read a book, or play a game of frisbee. Fitzgerald Park is more than simply a location; it's a pause button in the heart of Cork's fast-paced rhythm.

The Lough: A Tranquil Haven

A Reflection of the Sky

I went to The Lough, a magnificent freshwater lake that mirrors the sky and forms a calm refuge within the city limits, for a hidden jewel of tranquility. As I sat by the water's side, the smooth ripples and reflections of the surrounding trees painted a postcard-perfect sight.

Calm and Community

What distinguishes The Lough is its sense of community. Locals frequently come here for walks, jogging, or simply to enjoy the tranquil atmosphere.

Ducks and swans glide effortlessly over the pond, adding to the picturesque setting. Whether you want to be alone or have a calm conversation with a buddy, The Lough is a haven in the midst of the city.

Culinary Treats: From Pubs to Fine Dining

A Feast for the Senses

No visit to Cork would be complete without indulging in its culinary delights. Cork's food scene is a gastronomic trip ready to be appreciated, with everything from hearty pub fare to exquisite fine dining.

The Oliver Plunkett: Pints & Live Music

Irish Hospitality in a Pint Glass

The Oliver Plunkett, located in the heart of Cork, is a cultural institution as well as a pub. As soon as I came inside, the lively atmosphere and loud laughing of consumers made me feel like a member of the Cork family. The large assortment of Irish whiskeys and precisely poured pints provided a traditional Irish pub atmosphere.

Traditions and Foot-Tapping tunes

What distinguishes The Oliver Plunkett is its dedication to live music. Every night, the stage comes alive with traditional Irish tunes and contemporary music. As I thumped my foot to the beat and exchanged anecdotes with the locals, it became evident that The Oliver Plunkett is more than simply a pub; it's a tribute to Cork's musical past.

Farmgate Café: A Culinary Symphony in the English Market

Farm-to-Table Magic

The Farmgate Café in the heart of the English Market is a must-visit for a farm-to-table experience that tantalizes the taste buds. The intimate atmosphere, with its wooden tables and the buzz of market activity, is ideal for a gastronomic symphony.

Local Produce, Global Flavors

Farmgate Café's menu is a celebration of local products and world flavors. I loved a dish of substantial Irish stew cooked with ingredients acquired locally, as well as a beautiful pastry that melted in my lips. Farmgate Café is a gastronomic jewel amid the bustling market due to its commitment to excellence and combination of traditional Irish dishes with contemporary innovations.

Paradiso: Vegetarian Delights in a Culinary Oasis

A Haven for Vegetarian Gastronomy

Paradiso is a gourmet haven for those who appreciate vegetarian fare. This award-winning restaurant, tucked away on a quiet street, redefines vegetarian eating with its unique menu and commitment to sustainability.

Flavors that Dance on the Palate

I was astounded by the ingenuity on my plate when I dined on a multi-course meal at Paradiso. Each dish was transformed into a work of beauty by the flavors, textures, and presentation. Paradiso's culinary mastery made me realize the complexity and depth of vegetarian cuisine, from the rich, earthy tones of mushroom risotto to the vivid hues of roasted vegetable medley.

Epilogue: Cork - A Tapestry of Experiences Unveiled

I am going to forever take with me a tapestry of memories woven from the city's historical sites, green getaways, and culinary delights. Every cobblestone, every tune, and the warmth of Irish hospitality have permanent imprints on my journey.

Cork is more than just a place to visit; it's an entire experience that beckons you to dance through time, relish the flavors of the earth, and find peace in the embrace of natural areas. So, when you go off on your own Cork adventure, may your days be filled with the echoes of history, the serenity of nature, and the delightful symphony of flavors that make Cork a truly beautiful location.

Chapter 6

CULTURAL EXPERIENCES

Cork, with its rich history and lively vitality, emerges like a blank canvas waiting to be filled with artistic creations. Let's dive into the cultural tapestry that makes Cork a sanctuary for art fans, from classic work at the Crawford Art Gallery to fascinating performances at the Cork Opera House and the unique offers of the Triskel Arts Center.

Crawford Art Gallery: A Symphony of Artistic Epochs

Immersion in Art History

Entering the Crawford Art Gallery is like stepping into a time capsule of artistic eras. From classical treasures to modern works, this gallery is a must-see for art lovers. I became caught in the brushstrokes of famous artists and the stories spun by each beautifully arranged piece.

Art Beyond the Canvas

What distinguishes the Crawford Art Gallery is its dedication to make art accessible to everybody. The exhibitions range from classic paintings to sculptures, installations, and multimedia displays. As I moved through the galleries, each one told a different story, encouraging me to experience the world through the eyes of different artists and times.

Cork Opera House: Where the Stage Comes Alive

An Evening of Elegance

The Cork Opera House is a cultural jewel in the city's crown for a dose of performing arts. The refinement of the acts hosted within rivals the grandeur of the architecture. I saw an enthralling drama that transported me to another universe, and the acoustics during a musical performance were nothing short of hypnotic.

Versatility and variety

The adaptability of the Cork Opera House struck me the most. It is more than just a theater; it is a cultural center that hosts a wide range of performances. The theater comes alive with a varied range of artistic expressions, from live concerts and comedy plays to ballets and musicals. Examine the timetable; you might come upon anything that appeals to you.

Triskel Arts Center: A Bohemian Oasis

Artistic Vibes in a Historic Setting

The Triskel Arts Center, housed in a historic structure, is a bohemian haven that celebrates all forms of creativity. As I walked into the center, the eclectic environment immediately set the tone for a one-of-a-kind artistic experience. The combination of modern art installations, independent films, and live performances provides an immersive environment that entices the artistic soul.

Cinematic Adventures and Live Performances

One of the pleasures of my trip was seeing an indie film at the Triskel Cinema. The film selection, which is frequently beyond the popular circuit, provides a refreshing cinematic experience. Furthermore, the live performances in the Triskel Christchurch, a wonderfully renovated church, demonstrate the center's dedication to offering a platform for rising artists and unorthodox works.

Cultural Exploration: A Tapestry of Artistic Wonders

Cultural discovery in Cork is not limited to museums and theaters; it is a dynamic experience that unfolds in galleries, on stage, and in the city's bohemian enclaves. The Crawford Art Gallery, Cork Opera House, and Triskel Arts Center are more than just venues; they are doorways into Cork's cultural essence.

As you walk through these cultural sites, let the brushstrokes, songs, and performances weave a tapestry of amazement around you. Cultural encounters in Cork are about more than just seeing; they are about immersing yourself in the city's creative veins.

GASTRONOMIC ADVENTURES IN CORK

Prepare your taste buds for a gastronomic voyage around Cork's lovely culinary environment, my fellow food enthusiasts! Cork is a haven for those who appreciate the pleasures of fine food and drink, from the traditional warmth of Irish pubs to the exquisite flavors of local delicacies and the spirited world of whiskey distilleries.

Traditional Irish Pubs: Where Stories Flow Like Stout

The beating heart of Cork's social scene

Traditional Irish pubs are more than just venues to drink a pint; they are the social hub of Cork. The Oliver Plunkett is one such hidden gem, with an atmosphere as rich as the beers they pour. The murmur of friendly discussions and the lovely sounds of live Irish music produced an aura that seemed like a warm hug as I snuggled into the cozy room.

Perfectly poured pints and Irish cheer

The Oliver Plunkett has mastered the art of ordering a pint at an Irish pub. With its creamy head and velvety texture, the Guinness tasted like a sip of liquid history. The cordial discussion with locals, as well as the rhythmic rhythms of fiddles and bodhráns, enhanced the experience. It was more than just a drink; it was an expression of Irish spirit and friendship.

Culinary Delights: Farm-to-Table Magic in Cork

Exploring the English Market

The English Market is a culinary paradise that entices foodies with its brilliant colors and tantalizing fragrances. The Farmgate Café, nestled within, is a tribute to Cork's dedication to farm-to-table enchantment. I savored a traditional Irish breakfast, prepared with locally produced ingredients and served on a platter of culinary bliss. The symphony of tastes created by the sizzling bacon, flawlessly poached eggs, and handmade soda bread remained on my mouth.

A Paradiso Feast

Paradiso is a gourmet sanctuary tucked away on a quiet street for those looking for vegetarian delicacies. The restaurant's dedication to sustainability and inventive vegetarian cuisine astounded me. From the mushroom risotto to the roasted veggie medley, each dish was a work of art that displayed the richness and diversity of vegetarian cuisine. Paradiso is more than just a restaurant; it's a celebration of the beauty that can be accomplished without the use of meat.

Whiskey Distilleries: Spirited Explorations in Cork

A Whiskey Pilgrimage to Jameson Distillery

A visit to the Jameson Distillery is not complete without a stop in Cork. The aroma of aging whiskey barrels filled the air as I entered this iconic establishment, and educated guides guided me through the whiskey-making process. The tasting session took participants on a trip through the nuanced flavors of Jameson's finest, from the smooth Original to the rich complexity of the Reserve.

A Crafty Stop at The Dingle Whiskey Bar

The Dingle Whiskey Bar is a must-see for a more personal whiskey experience. This pub, housed in a historic structure, offers a broad selection of Irish and international whiskeys. I went on a tasting expedition to learn about the intricacies of various expressions. The bartender's knowledge and enthusiasm for whiskey converted the tasting into an educational and enjoyable excursion.

Culinary Revelations: Cork's Feast for the Senses

Gastronomic adventures in Cork are about more than just feeding your stomach; they are about indulging in a sensory feast that engages all of your senses. Cork's culinary scene is a voyage through Ireland's rich flavors and warm hospitality, from the conviviality of traditional Irish pubs to the culinary delights at the English Market and the vibrant world of whiskey distilleries.

So, while you explore Cork's culinary tapestry, let the flavors linger, the stories emerge, and the warmth of Irish hospitality accompany every bite and sip. Sláinte to the culinary adventures that await you in the heart of the Rebel City!

Chapter 7

SCENIC BEAUTY OF COUNTY CORK

We find ourselves immersed in the stunning scenery of County Cork as we travel beyond the quaint streets of Cork City. Let's discover the magnificent delights that await in this gorgeous part of Ireland, from the famed Ring of Kerry and the enchanting Skellig Islands to the historic Blarney Castle and the rough beauty of the Wild Atlantic Way.

Ring of Kerry: A Tapestry of Irish Landscapes

Killarney National Park: A Lush Green Paradise

Our first visit on the Ring of Kerry is the beautiful Killarney National Park. I was immersed by a symphony of colors the instant I stepped foot in this vast expanse - vivid greens of rolling hills, tranquil blues of lakes, and gentle hues of flowering wildflowers. The park is a paradise for nature lovers, with trails winding through ancient trees and across glistening lakes.

Visiting Muckross House

Muckross House, a Victorian mansion surrounded by magnificent gardens, is located in the heart of Killarney National Park. Exploring its sumptuous interiors took me to another age. The immaculate gardens are filled with brilliant blossoms and are ideal for a leisurely stroll. I couldn't pass up a traditional jaunting car ride, accompanied by a knowledgable guide whose stories provided a magical touch to the event.

Skellig Islands: An Atlantic Ocean Wonder

Our adventure continues to the enthralling Skellig Islands, which are a UNESCO World Heritage site. As our boat approached Skellig Michael, I was taken aback by the sight of old stone beehive cottages perched on the craggy cliffs. The islands are a haven for seabirds, and the air was filled with their sweet songs. Climbing to the monastery on Skellig Michael was a pilgrimage through history, with panoramic vistas of the Atlantic Ocean that will live on in my memory for the rest of my life.

Blarney Castle and Gardens

No trip to County Cork is complete without a stop at the renowned Blarney Castle. I couldn't get the thrill of kissing the renowned Blarney Stone out of my head as I ascended the castle's spiral staircase. The extensive gardens surrounding the castle provide a peaceful haven, complete with hidden passageways, blossoming flowers, and the calming sound of the River Martin.

Following the kissing ceremony, I investigated the Poison Garden, an intriguing variety of deadly plants that lent a sense of mystique to the encounter.

The Wild Atlantic Way: Rugged Beauty Unveiled

Clonakilty: Coastal Charms and Culinary Delights

Clonakilty is a jewel located along the Wild Atlantic Way, which unfolds with coastal delights. The town's colorful streets convey a bustling mood, and the smells of fresh seafood from local eateries tantalized my senses as I went around. The Michael Collins Centre provided insights into Ireland's revolutionary history, as well as a closer relationship to the coastal environments that surround Clonakilty.

Mizen Head: Ireland's Southernmost Point

Mizen Head, Ireland's southernmost point, was a picturesque highlight. The Atlantic Ocean stretched out in front of me, creating a stunning symphony of breaking waves against the craggy cliffs. The historic Mizen Bridge, perched above the roiling seas, provided an exciting vantage position. Exploring the Mizen Signal Station, poised on the cliff's edge, afforded a look into this distant outpost's maritime history.

Beara Peninsula: A Hidden Haven

The Beara Peninsula revealed its hidden delights as our trek along the Wild Atlantic Way progressed. I passed through quaint villages, ancient stone circles, and landscapes that seemed to exist in harmony with time as I drove down the meandering roads. Dursey Island, reached by Ireland's lone cable car, felt like another world. The peace and quiet of the peninsula, away from the busy tourist routes, allowed me to absorb the true essence of Ireland's untamed and untouched beauty.

Fota Wildlife Park: A Safari in Ireland

Our next stop is to Fota Wildlife Park, a one-of-a-kind safari adventure in the heart of County Cork. The sense of absorption in natural environments as I went across the park was unequaled. Every encounter, from the curious lemurs to the majestic cheetahs, felt like a window into the world's different ecosystems. The Asian Sanctuary, which is home to tigers and Indian rhinoceros, served as a heartbreaking reminder of the value of conservation efforts.

A Symphony of Scenic Wonders: Cork's Natural Masterpieces

County Cork, with its magnificent delights, is a nature lover's paradise. Each site unveils as a natural masterpiece, from the beautiful landscapes of the Ring of Kerry to the historic attraction of Blarney Castle and the wild beauty of the Wild Atlantic Way.

As I ponder on my voyage across County Cork's stunning grandeur, I'm reminded that Ireland's genuine allure rests not only in its towns, but also in the pristine landscapes that whisper tales of ancient history and unending beauty.

Sláinte to the magnificent wonders that greet every traveler in County Cork!

Chapter 8

OUTDOOR ACTIVITIES

Prepare to lace up your boots, grab a paddle, swing a club, and cycle your way across the breathtaking landscapes that make Cork a refuge for outdoor enthusiasts as we explore the wonderful outdoors of County Cork.

Let's explore the numerous ways you can appreciate County Cork's natural playground, from the rough paths of Sheeps Head Peninsula to the exhilarating water sports choices and the stunning golf courses.

Hiking and Trekking

Sheeps Head Peninsula: A Hiker's Paradise

I found myself enveloped in a patchwork of rolling hills, rugged cliffs, and coastal routes that beckon hikers of all levels when I ventured into the Sheeps Head Peninsula. A recognized trail, the Sheeps Head Way, provides panoramic views of Bantry Bay and the untamed Atlantic. The saline breeze and the sound of seagulls accompanied my stroll over the rough shoreline. The peacefulness of the landscape made it a hike to remember.

Encounters with Wildlife

Seeing seals sunning on the rocks below was one of the pleasures. These strange critters seemed unafraid of my presence, creating a magical link with the surrounding nature. The path took me through picturesque villages where kind inhabitants told me stories about the peninsula's history, offering a cultural layer to my outdoor trip.

The Ballyhoura Mountains: Peaks and Valleys to Conquer

The Ballyhoura Mountains welcomed me with open arms for a more difficult trip. The route system here is ideal for both hikers and mountain bikers. The patchwork quilt of lush meadows and deep forests unfurled beneath me as I reached the hills. The exciting descent through wooded valleys only added to the sensation of success at the peak.

Water Sports: Riding the Waves and Sailing the Seas

Kayaking and Canoeing: Gliding Through Cork's Waterways

Cork's rivers provide a haven for kayakers and canoeists. The River Lee, which runs through the city, is a great place to start. I rented a kayak and paddled around the riverbanks, passing under old bridges and appreciating the city from a different vantage point. The river's tranquil flow helped me to reconnect with nature right in the heart of Cork.

Surfing: Riding Atlantic Swells

The Atlantic shoreline is ideal for individuals looking for an adrenaline boost. With its gorgeous sands and dependable waves, Inchydoney Beach became my surfing refuge. The exhilaration of paddling into the Atlantic swells and catching my first wave was nothing short of amazing. Surf schools along the coast offer introductory lessons, making surfing an accessible adventure for anyone.

Sailing: Navigating the Atlantic Breeze

Cork's harbors and bays are a sailing enthusiast's dream. Kinsale, with its vibrant waterfront, was my sailing base. I rented a boat and set sail into the Atlantic breeze, past rocky cliffs and quiet bays. As I cruised the same seas historically sailed by traders and explorers, the region's nautical history came to life.

Golfing: Swinging in the Green Splendor

Top Golf Courses in Cork: A Golfer's Paradise

Cork has some of the best golf courses in Ireland, situated against the beautiful greenery of the countryside. The Old Head Golf Links, located on a promontory surrounded by stunning cliffs, provided a unique golfing experience. Every swing became a ballet between perfection and the beautiful surroundings as I teed off overlooking the Atlantic.

Kinsale Golf Club, located on Ireland's picturesque southern shore, offered a more casual but equally pleasant game. The well-kept fairways and scenic scenery made every stroke a delight. Cork's golf courses cater to all skill levels, ensuring an enjoyable day on the green whether you're a seasoned golfer or a novice.

Cycling Routes: Pedaling Through Cork's Landscapes

The Great Southern Trail: A Cycling Odyssey

The Great Southern Trail is a scenic path that winds through County Limerick and County Kerry for cyclists. My voyage began at Newcastle West, and the sense of calm was obvious as I pedaled through gorgeous woodlands and past antique railway stations. The relatively level and well-maintained track is appropriate for cyclists of all abilities.

Beara Peninsula Cycling: A Coastal Adventure

Cycling the Beara Peninsula was a coastal excursion that revealed Ireland's southwest's rough beauty. The path followed the shore, providing beautiful views of the Atlantic. I had the opportunity to stop at local cafés and bars as I drove through picturesque villages, immersing myself in the wonderful welcome of the coastal communities.

Nature's Playground: A Symphony of Outdoor Activities

Nature transforms County Cork into a large playground, inviting visitors to trek along gorgeous trails, ride the waves of the Atlantic, swing clubs on world-class golf courses, and pedal through scenic landscapes. From the calm Sheeps Head Peninsula to the adrenaline-pumping surf of Inchydoney Beach, each outdoor activity in Cork's natural paradise emerges as a symphony of adventure.

So, when you set out on your outdoor adventures in County Cork, may each walk, paddle, swing, and pedal bring you closer to the heart of Ireland's wild beauty. Sláinte to the wide outdoors and the myriad experiences that await you in Rebel County!

Chapter 9

DAY TRIPS FROM CORK

Let's continue our Cork tour by sailing to the picturesque towns and historical treasures that surround the Rebel City.

These day trips promise a rich tapestry of history, culture, and culinary experiences beyond the city limits, from the Titanic connections of Cobh to the gourmet joys of Kinsale, the whiskey wonders of Midleton, and the birthplace of a revolutionary icon in Clonakilty.

Cobh - The Titanic Connection: A Journey Back in Time

Cobh Heritage Center: Echoes of Maritime History

Our first day trip takes us to Cobh, a charming town rich in maritime history and, importantly, the last port of call for the ill-fated Titanic. The Cobh Heritage Center acted as my time machine. Walking around its interactive exhibits, I learned about the Titanic's passengers, the Lusitania's tragedies, and the consequences of Irish emigration.

Embracing the Titanic Legacy

Cobh's connection to the Titanic is strong, and the Titanic Experience at the center accurately recreated the atmosphere of the ship's departure. Standing on the same wharf where passengers earlier said their goodbyes, I felt a strong connection to this watershed moment in history. The personal accounts, relics, and immersive exhibits took me to a time of big ocean ships and daring adventures.

Spike Island: A Historical Fortress

Spike Island, a medieval fortress with layers of intriguing history, was a short boat journey from Cobh. The guided tour revealed centuries of history, from its beginnings as a monastic colony to its evolution into a formidable military fortress. While walking through the jail cells, I learned about the island's darker history, including its use as a convict depot.

Journey Through Military History

As I explored the star-shaped castle and heard stories of battles and strategic importance, Spike Island's military history came to life. The panoramic views of Cork Harbor from the highest point on the island were nothing short of magnificent. Spike Island is more than just a historical place; it is a multidimensional trip through time, integrating victory and tribulation stories.

Kinsale, Ireland's Gourmet Capital: A Culinary Odyssey

Charles Fort: A Historical Relic

Our next expedition brings us to Kinsale, Ireland's Gourmet Capital. A tour to Charles Fort provided an enthralling peek into Kinsale's military history before indulging in culinary delicacies. Perched on a hill overlooking the harbor, the star-shaped stronghold provided panoramic views of the town and the sea.

A Journey Through Time

Wandering through Charles Fort's battlements and underground rooms led me to several eras, from 17th-century military strategy to 20th-century expansions during the Irish Civil War. Charles Fort's historical significance, paired with its gorgeous position, made it an ideal forerunner to the culinary delights that awaited in Kinsale.

Foodie Tours: A Palate Feast

Kinsale's status as the Gourmet Capital is well-deserved, and a gastronomic tour turned out to be the highlight of my trip. Each stop on the tour introduced me to the town's lively culinary sector, from artisanal cheese shops to seafood markets. Tastings of regional specialties, such as fresh seafood, handcrafted chocolates, and savory pastries, provided a sensory overload.

Savouring Gourmet Delights

Kinsale's eateries enticed me with Michelin-starred places and charming bars. The marriage of traditional Irish flavors and modern culinary methods was a gourmet journey. The town's cobblestone alleys dotted with colorful buildings made for a wonderful setting for a leisurely stroll following a sumptuous supper.

Midleton - Home of Jameson Distillery: A Whiskey Pilgrimage

The Jameson Experience: Unveiling the Whiskey Craft

A day journey to Midleton, home of the Jameson Distillery, is a pilgrimage into the world of Irish whiskey for whiskey fans. The Jameson Experience offers an interactive experience through the whiskey-making process, situated in a refurbished 19th-century distillery. Every stage, from malting to maturing, was revealed with accuracy and enthusiasm.

Tasting the Liquid Gold

The whiskey tasting session, when I sampled a variety of Jameson's finest, was the tour's high point. From the smooth Original to the rich intricacy of the Reserve, the experienced guide walked me through the nuances of each expression. Tasting the liquid gold in the location where it was created provided an extra dimension of appreciation to each sip.

The Old Midleton Distillery: A Journey Through Time

The Old Midleton Distillery, adjacent to the present distillery, is a protected time capsule that allows tourists to travel back in time. Exploring the old buildings, cooperage, and warehouses provided insights into Irish whiskey production's heritage. The perfume of aging barrels and the creaking of wooden flooring contributed to the realistic atmosphere.

A Toast to Irish Whiskey Heritage

Midleton is more than just a whiskey destination; it's a celebration of Ireland's whiskey heritage. The blending of tradition and modernity, as displayed through interactive exhibits and tastings, made the Jameson Distillery a must-see for anybody interested in the craft of whiskey making.

Clonakilty - Birthplace of Michael Collins: A Revolutionary Legacy

Our final day journey brings us to Clonakilty, the birthplace of Michael Collins, a pivotal figure in Ireland's independence war. The picturesque alleys and ancient sites in town give tribute to this revolutionary leader.

Immersion in History at the Michael Collins Center

The Michael Collins Center, located in West Cork's countryside, is a fascinating site for history buffs. The displays and performances at the center describe Michael Collins' life, from his infancy in Clonakilty to his vital involvement in the Irish independence struggle. The interactive displays and multimedia presentations bring history to life, forging a strong bond with Ireland's revolutionary past.

Exploring Clonakilty's Charms

Clonakilty, beyond the Michael Collins Center, provides a magnificent location for exploration. The lively streets of the town are lined with colorful shops, classic bars, and pleasant cafes. I could feel the echoes of the past mingled with the bustling mood of the present as I went around the old square.

A Day Trip Through Time and Taste

Clonakilty combines history and culture in a town that reflects Ireland's revolutionary spirit. Every moment seemed like a journey through time and taste, from understanding Michael Collins' life to meandering through gorgeous streets.

Day Trips Revealed: Cork's Surrounding Treasures

As our day visits progressed, each town showed a different aspect of Cork's varied heritage. These day visits provided depth and complexity to my Cork vacation, from the nautical echoes of Cobh and the foodie delights of Kinsale to the whiskey wonders of Midleton and the revolutionary past of Clonakilty.

So, when you begin on these Cork day tours, may each historical place, gastronomic experience, and cultural contact become a treasured chapter in your Irish voyage.

Chapter 10

CORK FOR FAMILIES

Cork, with its rich history and dynamic culture, is ideal for families as well as solo travelers and couples. Cork offers a wholesome blend of fun and learning for families, from agricultural excursions and island escapades to educational delights. Join me as we explore the family-friendly sights and educational experiences that make Cork a great family vacation destination.

Family-Friendly Attractions: Where Fun Knows No Age

Leahy's Open Farm: A Day on the Farm

Leahy's Open Farm is a refuge for families looking for a fun day out in nature with farm animals. The excitement on children's faces as they engaged with friendly animals was contagious as I strolled through the verdant fields. The farm experience was a fantastic blend of amusement and knowledge, with everything from lamb feeding to pony rides.

Animal Encounters and Playgrounds for Adventure

The open farm is home to a wide range of animals, including frisky goats and elegant peacocks. My children were able to get up close and personal with their furry friends thanks to the petting area, which fostered a sense of connection with the animal realm. The adventure playgrounds, complete with slides and climbing frames, introduced a new layer of excitement to Leahy's Open Farm, transforming it into a full-fledged family experience.

Fota Island Adventure: A Wildlife Expedition

Our next family-friendly adventure led us to Fota Wildlife Park on Fota Island, a wildlife enthusiast's paradise for all ages. The park's unconventional strategy of allowing animals to roam freely in big enclosures created an immersive experience that felt more like a safari than a standard zoo.

Roaming with the Animals

The sight of giraffes grazing in the distance and lemurs playing in the treetops made every step an experience as we walked through the park. The open architecture of the enclosures brought my family closer to the animals, and the park rangers' educational speeches provided intriguing insights into conservation efforts and wildlife behavior.

Blackrock Castle Observatory: Galactic Discoveries

A trip to Blackrock Castle Observatory was an excellent alternative for families with budding astronomers. Perched on the banks of the Lee River, the castle combines history with cutting-edge science exhibits and interactive displays.

Exploring the universe

We began on a cosmic voyage within the observatory. The planetarium displays took us to distant galaxies, while the hands-on exhibits allowed us to learn about our solar system's wonders. The highlight was looking up at the night sky through telescopes, with professional astronomers taking us through celestial discoveries. Blackrock Castle Observatory transformed space exploration into an exciting excursion for the entire family.

Educational Experiences: Where Learning is Fun

Lifetime Lab: A Scientific Journey

The Lifetime Lab, located in the historic setting of the Old Cork Waterworks, is a science center that perfectly integrates teaching with hands-on pleasure.

The exhibits include a wide spectrum of scientific topics, making it a fun experience for people of all ages.

Exploration of Science through Play

My family and I had a great time interacting with interactive displays, learning about physics, and even learning about environmental sustainability.

The outdoor playground's water-themed activities brought a joyful aspect to the educational experience. The Lifetime Lab's dedication to making science approachable and pleasant made it popular with both parents and children.

Cork City Gaol Heritage Center: A History Lesson

The Cork City Gaol Heritage Center provided a fascinating voyage back in time for families interested in history. The massive castle-like structure, which was previously a jail, today remains as a reminder of Ireland's violent history.

Historical Reenactments and Educational Exhibits

We learned about the life of convicts and the social history of Ireland in the nineteenth and early twentieth centuries as we walked through the cold, echoing corridors.

The historical reenactments, replete with costumed guides, gave the tour a theatrical flair. The exhibits inside the center provided fascinating insights into the hardships and successes of Ireland's drive for independence.

Cork: A Family-Friendly Destination

Cork's options for family-friendly activities are as varied as the city itself. Cork invites families to study, play, and make lifelong memories together, from open farms and wildlife parks to science institutes and historical places.

As I saw the children's smiles and shared moments of discovery, it became clear that Cork is more than simply a destination; it's a family-friendly paradise where fun knows no age.

Pack your curiosity, passion, and sense of wonder, fellow family explorers, as you embark on a family-friendly journey through Cork. Each attraction and educational experience should serve as a stepping stone in your family's vacation, forming ties and memories that will last a lifetime.

Sláinte to family fun in the Rebel City!

Chapter 11

NIGHTLIFE AND ENTERTAINMENT

Cork's after-dark culture is a tapestry of experiences, ranging from old pubs ringing with Irish music to sophisticated cocktail bars mixing up inventive concoctions and theater stages lit up for live performances. Join me as we explore the nocturnal joys of Cork's nightlife, visiting the pubs, theaters, and nightclubs that make the city's nightlife an amazing adventure.

Pubs and Bars: A Toast to Traditions and Innovations

Traditional Irish Music: A Symphony in the Pubs

Cork's nightlife cannot be discussed without mentioning its rich legacy of Irish music. The comfortable interiors and welcoming atmospheres of the pubs serve as stages for impromptu sessions of fiddles, bodhráns, and soul-stirring singing.

The Warm Hues of Traditional Pubs

My introduction to the traditional music culture in Cork began in cozy pubs like The Oliver Plunkett and An Spailpn Fánach. The warm tones of the wooden interiors, the clinking of glasses, and the rhythmic tapping of feet all contributed to the lively atmosphere.

The musicians transported me to a realm where time appeared to stop still while I sipped a pint of Guinness, and the stories woven into each melody presented a vivid picture of Ireland's cultural history.

Trendy Cocktail Bars: Mixology Magic in Modern Settings

Cork has a number of hip cocktail establishments that redefine mixology for those looking for a more modern ambiance. The city's mixologists, armed with ingenuity and a flair for the theatrical, create visually spectacular as well as delectable cocktails.

Cocktail Adventures in the City

I found myself engaged in a realm of mixology magic after entering the trendy Cask. The menu was a piece of art in and of itself, with unique flavor combinations and premium drinks. With the clinking of ice and the gentle murmur of voices, the darkly lit environment formed an intimate backdrop for a night of cocktail experiences.

Theatres and Live Performances: A Stage for Every Story

Cork Opera House: Elegance and Grandeur

Cork's cultural lifeblood pulsates through its theaters, and the Cork Opera House is a tribute to the city's passion for the performing arts. With its beautiful architecture and regal presence, this historic venue showcases a wide spectrum of live entertainment.

Cultural Shows Under the Chandeliers

A night at the Cork Opera House was an evening of elegance and cultural immersion. The majestic chandeliers, luxurious velvet chairs, and buzz in the air produced an ambiance reminiscent of the golden age of theatre. Every show was a voyage into the core of artistic expression, from world-class plays to musical performances that crossed genres.

Everyman Theatre: Intimacy and Artistry

The Everyman Theatre emerged as a hidden gem in the heart of Cork for a more intimate theatrical experience. The red-brick exterior and tiny auditorium set the tone for evenings of humor, drama, and heartbreaking moments.

A Platform for Diverse Narratives

I was drawn to the Everyman Theatre because of its commitment to presenting various storytelling. The theatre's programming catered to a wide range of tastes, from thought-provoking dramas to side-splitting comedies. The intimacy with the performers and the shared experience with the audience fostered a sense of community that made each visit to the Everyman Theatre unique.

Nightclubs & Late-Night venues: Dancing Until Dawn

Cork's nightclubs and late-night establishments cater to individuals who enjoy letting loose and dancing the night away, with throbbing sounds and an electric environment that keeps the party going into the early hours.

A Dance Floor Odyssey

Cyprus Avenue and Havana Browns were buzzing with the energy of Cork's nightlife. With their cutting-edge sound systems and explosive DJ sets, these hotspots became my dance floor trip. The eclectic combination of music, from chart-toppers to underground sounds, catered to a wide range of tastes, ensuring that the dance floor was a hive of energy.

The Allure of Late-Night Adventures

Late-night places like The Hanover and The Woodford became havens for individuals looking for a more laid-back yet energetic setting as the night progressed. The quiet corners and ambient lighting created the ideal setting for talks that flowed as easily as the drinks.

A Night to Remember in Cork

Cork's nightlife is a tapestry of experiences that weave together the old and the contemporary, the cultural and the throbbing pulses of the night. I learned that Cork's nightlife is as diverse as the city itself as I traveled through pubs throbbing with Irish tunes, drank on handmade cocktails in sophisticated bars, experienced compelling shows in theaters, and danced under the neon lights of nightclubs.

So, fellow night owls and cultural enthusiasts, may each pub tune, drink sip, theatrical performance, and dancing move become a bright brush in your own canvas of Cork memories as you explore Cork's nightlife. Sláinte to nights full with laughter, rhythm, and the enchantment of Cork at night!

Chapter 12

PRACTICAL INFORMATION

As we near the end of our tour of the Rebel City, let's look at some practical tips for making the most of your time in Cork. Let's look at the practical knowledge that will improve your entire Cork experience, from understanding the local currency to embracing cultural etiquette and prioritizing health and safety.

Currency and Banking: Managing Your Finances

Understanding the local currency and banking is essential for a smooth stay in Cork.

The Euro as a Currency: Coins and Bills in Ireland

Cork, like the rest of Ireland, has an official currency of the Euro (€). The Euro is divided into coins and bills, with coins ranging from one cent to two euros and bills ranging from five to five hundred euros. Although cash is frequently accepted, credit and debit cards are also widely utilized, particularly in urban areas.

Banking Services: Cork ATMs and Banks

ATMs, sometimes called locally as "cash points," are located around Cork, making it easy to withdraw cash. In shops, restaurants, and hotels, major credit and debit cards are frequently accepted. Monday through Friday, with some branches open on Saturdays. To avoid problems with card transactions abroad, notify your bank of your travel dates.

Emergency Services: Prioritizing Safety

Knowing how to contact emergency services is critical for your safety and well-being while in Cork.

Emergency Numbers: 999 and 112

In an emergency, phone 999 or 112 to reach the necessary services, such as police, fire, medical help, or search and rescue. These are toll-free numbers that can be called from any phone, including mobile phones.

Medical Emergencies: Cork University Hospital and Local Clinics

Cork University Hospital (CUH) is the city's largest medical center, capable of handling a wide range of medical crises. Local clinics and general practitioners (GPs) are also available for non-emergency medical needs. Travel insurance that covers medical bills and emergencies is recommended.

Local Etiquette and Customs: Embracing Irish Hospitality

Understanding local manners and customs promotes productive interactions with Cork's welcoming residents.

Politeness and Friendliness: The Irish Way

Irish people are recognized for their friendliness and warmth. Simply saying "please" and "thank you" goes a long way toward expressing politeness. Small talk is prevalent among locals, so don't be shocked if someone strikes up a conversation with you in a tavern or café.

Personal Space: A Considerate Approach

While Irish people are generally cordial, they value personal space. Queues are prevalent in public places, so patiently wait your time. A polite smile and nod are frequently sufficient greetings.

Dining Etiquette: Tipping and Pub Culture

Tipping is prevalent at restaurants, with a normal tip of 10-15% of the total. It is customary in pubs to order and pay at the bar. If someone offers to buy you a drink, it is customary to reciprocate the gesture.

Language and Communication: Interacting with the Locals

The official language of Cork is English, however the Irish language (Gaeilge) is officially recognized and taught in schools.

English as the Primary Language: Communicating Effectively

English is the most commonly spoken language in Cork, and the residents are fluent and kind to visitors. The street signs, menus, and public information are all in English, making it simple for visitors to get around.

Gaelic Phrases: A Cultural Touch

While English is the primary language, hearing a few Gaelic phrases might enhance your cultural experience. "Dia dhuit" (Hello) and "Sláinte" (Cheers) are widespread and valued greetings.

Health and Safety: Prioritizing Well-Being

For a worry-free exploration of Cork, keep health and safety in mind.

Medical Facilities: Cork University Hospital and Pharmacies

Cork University Hospital (CUH) is a comprehensive medical center that can address a wide range of medical conditions. Furthermore, pharmacies (chemists) are located throughout the city and offer over-the-counter pharmaceuticals as well as basic healthcare supplies.

Vaccinations: General Health Precautions

There are no special immunizations necessary to enter Ireland, although it is recommended that routine vaccinations be up to date. Consult your healthcare professional before flying if you have any special health concerns or conditions.

Finally: A Well-Informed Cork Adventure

As we end our examination of Cork, equipped with useful information, you are now ready to immerse yourself in the Rebel City's rich culture, exciting nightlife, and welcoming attitude. Cork is a location that blends heritage and contemporary charm, from the cobblestone lanes of its ancient center to the vibrant pubs ringing with traditional tunes and the modern comforts that ensure your comfort.

So, fellow visitors, may your time in Cork be full with fascinating discoveries, friendly interactions, and the excitement of seeing a city that perfectly blends the past and the present. Sláinte to an exciting and memorable adventure in Cork, Ireland!

Chapter 13

RESOURCES AND TRAVEL TIPS

As we near the end of our Cork adventure, let's look at the details that can elevate your journey from good to outstanding. These tools will act as your compass in the Rebel City, from crucial websites and applications to local information centers and travel guides.

Useful Websites and Apps: Your Digital Travel Companions

Travel Apps for Efficient Exploration

Cork is a city that perfectly blends its rich history with modern conveniences, and your smartphone might be your finest companion in exploring its allure. Apps like "Cork City Guide" provide in-depth information about sites, events, and local recommendations. "Transport for Ireland" is useful for public transit timetables, while "Cork Like" will help you find hidden gems popular among locals. Having these apps at your fingertips makes it easier to explore the city.

Websites for Comprehensive Information

Perusing relevant websites before beginning on your Cork vacation can provide valuable insights. "Visit Cork" provides an in-depth reference to sights, events, and practical information. "Pure Cork" is a great place to get real-time updates about events and festivals. Furthermore, staying up to date on local news via websites like "The Irish Times" ensures you're aware of any developments that may affect your vacation.

Local Tourist Information Centers: Navigating with Expertise

Cork Tourist Information Centers

Cork has various tourist information centers that serve as knowledge centers for travelers. The main Tourist Information Office on Grand Parade is a treasure mine of leaflets, maps, and helpful staff. There are also information points at crucial areas such as the airport and rail station. These centers provide more than simply maps; they also provide access to local insights and recommendations.

Guidance from Local Experts

Getting in touch with the experts at tourist information centers can provide vital assistance. They can help you customize your itinerary based on your interests, propose hidden treasures, and keep you up to date on events taking place during your visit. These centers are your direct link to local expertise, whether you're looking for the best pub for traditional music or off-the-beaten-path attractions.

Cork Travel Tips: Enhancing Your Experience

Saving Money: Budget-Friendly Adventures

Cork is a city that welcomes all types of visitors, including those on a tight budget. To make the most of your money, consider purchasing a "Cork Card," which provides discounts on attractions, tours, and eating. Exploring local markets for fresh produce can also be a cost-effective way to enjoy wonderful meals. Many bars and restaurants also offer early bird discounts, allowing you to indulge in gastronomic delights at a lower cost.

Navigating Public Transportation

Taking public transit is not only environmentally friendly, but also cost effective. The city's bus network is large, and the Leap Card makes it easy to pay for your trips. Exploring the region by train or bus offers scenic routes and cost-effective possibilities for day getaways. Planning your mobility ahead of time and taking advantage of bundled attraction tickets can result in big savings.

Sustainable Travel: Treading Lightly in Cork

Cork, with its verdant landscapes and commitment to sustainability, invites visitors to explore while leaving a small environmental legacy.

Eco-Friendly Accommodations and Dining

Choosing accommodation that prioritizes sustainability might improve your travel experience. Cork has a variety of eco-friendly hotels that emphasize energy efficiency, trash reduction, and community involvement. Similarly, eating at restaurants that source locally and promote sustainability benefits the community while also providing a unique taste of Cork's culinary scene.

Exploring by Bike and Foot

Cork's tiny city center is ideal for exploring on foot, since it allows you to absorb in the atmosphere and find hidden jewels. Renting a bike is not only a sustainable option for a more active approach, but it is also a terrific opportunity to journey outside the city center and visit the scenic environs.

Responsible Tourism: Leaving a Positive Impact

Respecting the local culture, environment, and community is part of being a responsible traveler in Cork.

Cultural respect and Sensitivity

Embracing the local culture is more than just observing; it also entails honoring customs and engaging in respectful interactions with the community. When visiting historical places, follow the rules and avoid activities that could jeopardize preservation efforts. Engaging with residents with an open mind and curiosity leads to beneficial interactions and a better grasp of the city's history.

Supporting Local Businesses and Artisans

Cork has a thriving community of local craftspeople, ranging from craftsmen to small boutiques. Purchasing souvenirs from local companies not only assures you take home one-of-a-kind treasures, but also directly supports to the livelihoods of Cork's creative community. Each purchase becomes a piece of Cork's story, whether it's handmade jewelry, traditional crafts, or locally produced goods.

Waste Reduction and Responsible Disposal

Being careful of trash is part of reducing your environmental effect. Cork promotes appropriate garbage disposal by providing clearly designated recycling bins in public areas. Reduced usage of single-use plastics and increased use of reusable alternatives add to the city's commitment to sustainability.

Closing Thoughts: A Thoughtful Cork Odyssey

As we finish our journey into the heart of Cork, armed with useful information and travel advice, I hope your adventure is more than just a collection of experiences, but a purposeful exploration that leaves a good mark. Cork, with its unique blend of history, culture, and modernity, invites us to be mindful tourists who embrace the essence of responsible tourism.

May your time in Cork be full with discoveries, connections, and memories that will last long after you leave the Rebel City. Sláinte to a thoughtful and wonderful Cork journey!

Appendix

CRAFTING YOUR CORK ADVENTURE

This section has a wealth of additional information, ranging from carefully created sample itineraries to a useful traveler's checklist and even a glossary of typical Irish phrases to lend a touch of Gaelic charm to your interactions.

Let's go into the specifics so your Cork journey is as rewarding as possible.

Sample Itineraries: Tailoring Your Cork Experience

Weekend Getaway: A Taste of Cork's Charm

Day 1: Unveiling the City's Heart

- Morning: Start your adventure by strolling down St. Patrick's Street. At a neighborhood café, savor a typical Irish breakfast.
- Afternoon: Visit the Cork City Gaol Heritage Center and immerse yourself in history. Grab a bite to eat at the historic English Market.
- Evening: Visit Shandon's cultural haven, climb the Shandon Bells, and watch the sunset at Elizabeth Fort.
- At night, explore the city's nightlife on Oliver Plunkett Street while listening to traditional Irish music.

Day 2: Scenic Beauty and Coastal Magic

- Morning: Take a lovely drive around the Ring of Kerry. Take a trip through Killarney National Park.
- Afternoon: Have lunch in the charming village of Kenmare. Continue driving to get a better view of the Skellig Islands.
- Return to Cork in the evening and lunch at one of the waterfront restaurants.

One Week in Cork: A Comprehensive Tour

Day 1-2: Cork City Delights

- St. Patrick's Street, the English Market, and the ancient Cork City Gaol are all worth seeing.
- Visit Shandon for panoramic vistas and the famous Shandon Bells. On Oliver Plunkett Street, immerse yourself in the city's nightlife.

Day 3-4: County Cork's Scenic Wonders

- Explore Killarney National Park and the lovely village of Kenmare on the Ring of Kerry.
- Discover the Beara Peninsula's rocky beauty and the seaside splendor of Mizen Head.

Day 5-6: Outdoor Adventures and Day Trips

- Hike the Ballyhoura Mountains or the Sheeps Head Peninsula.
- Take part in water sports in Clonakilty or learn about Cobh's maritime history.

Day 7: Family-Friendly Fun

- Spend the day at Fota Wildlife Park and then head to the city for a family-friendly lunch.

Family Adventure: Memorable Moments in Cork

Day 1: Leahy's Open Farm and Family Time

- Morning: Visit Leahy's Open Farm to get a taste of farm life.
- Afternoon: Have lunch at the farm and let the kids play on the adventure playgrounds.
- Evening: Return to town for a family meal.

Day 2: Fota Wildlife Park Expedition

- Morning: Visit Fota Wildlife Park and see exotic creatures.
- Afternoon: Have a picnic at the park and play in the playground.
- Evening: Spend the evening relaxing in the city.

Day 3: Educational Explorations

- Morning: Explore science hands-on at the Lifetime Lab.
- Afternoon: Visit the Cork City Gaol Heritage Center and have lunch in the city.
- Evening: Dine at a family-friendly restaurant.

Traveler's Checklist: Cork Essentials for Cork Journey

Before You Go:

- Passport and visa (if applicable)
- Travel protection insurance
- Reservations for flights and accommodations
- Cork and surrounding area maps, both printed and digital
- Weather-appropriate attire

Packing Essentials:

- Comfortable walking shoes
- Weather-appropriate clothing (layering is essential)
- Power adapters for electronic gadgets
- Portable charger
- Camera or smartphone for capturing memories
- Reusable water bottle

Financial Preparedness:

- Cash in local currency (Euros)
- Credit/debit cards with travel notifications
- Keep emergency cash in a safe place

Health and safety:

- Prescriptions and personal medications
- Basic first aid kit
- Toiletries in travel-size
- insect repellant
- Sunglasses and sunscreen

Tech and connectivity:

- Smartphone with important travel apps
- Portable charger for on-the-go recharging
- Travel-sized electronics such as a tablet or e-reader

Local Knowledge:

- Learn a few common Irish phrases (see Glossary).
- Familiarize yourself with local emergency numbers

- Know the location of the nearest tourist information center.

Glossary of Common Irish Phrases: Embracing the Local Lingo

Greetings and Pleasantries:

- "Dia dhuit" - Hello
- "Slán" - Goodbye
- "Go raibh maith agat" - Thank you

Social Interactions:

- "Craic" - Fun or enjoyable time
- "Céad míle fáilte" - A hundred thousand welcomes
- "Álainn" - Beautiful

Dining and Drinking:

- "Sláinte" - Cheers

- "Go maith" - Good
- "Bain sult as do bhéile" - Enjoy your meal

Directions and Navigation:

- "Anseo" - Here
- "Amach anseo" - Out here
- "Ansin" - There

Closing Thoughts: Embarking on Your Cork Odyssey

May your Cork tour be full with joy, discovery, and experiences that endure long after you say goodbye to the Rebel City, armed with these sample itineraries, crucial checklists, and a sprinkle of Irish vocabulary. Cork is more than just a place to visit; it's an entire experience that combines history, culture, and the warmth of Irish hospitality. Sláinte to your Cork adventure, and may it be a chapter in your travel journey that you can look back on with a smile!

Index

NAVIGATING CORK'S RICH TAPESTRY

Let us take a moment to navigate this thorough index as we conclude our adventure across Cork. This index is your guide to the best sites to visit, cozy lodging alternatives, tasty food options, exhilarating activities, and useful information to make the most of your trip.

So, let's get started and discover the hidden jewels that Cork has to offer.

Places of Interest: Cork's Charms Unveiled

Cork City Center: A Traditional and Modern Tapestry

- **St. Patrick's Street:** Cork's vibrant hub, dotted with shops, cafes, and historic sites.
- **The English Market:** A foodie's dream with fresh produce and handcrafted delights.
- **Cork City Gaol:** Immerse yourself in history by visiting this magnificent former prison turned museum.

Cork's Historical Landmarks: Echoes of the Past

- **Cork City Hall:** A work of art with guided tours and breathtaking vistas.

- **Shandon Bells and Tower:** Climb the tower for panoramic views and a historical lesson about bell-ringing.
- **Elizabeth Fort:** A military fortress with spectacular city views.

Cultural Experiences: Art, Music, and Performance

- **Crawford Art Gallery:** With constantly changing exhibitions, you can immerse yourself in Cork's lively art scene.
- **Cork Opera House:** A cultural destination for everything from theater to live music.
- **Triskel Arts Center:** A multimodal arts venue that hosts cinema screenings, concerts, and visual arts.

Gastronomic Adventures: Savoring Cork's Flavors

- **Traditional Irish Pubs**: In the city's traditional pubs, you may experience the warmth of Irish hospitality.
- **Culinary Delights:** From seafood to artisanal cheese, discover Cork's eclectic gastronomic culture.
- **Whiskey distilleries:** Tours and tastings are available to learn about the craft of manufacturing whiskey.

Accommodation Options: Relaxing Retreats in Cork

Hotels: Luxury and Convenience

- **The River Lee Hotel:** A riverfront hotel with modern amenities and a spa.

- **Hayfield Manor:** a five-star haven with exquisite suites and magnificent gardens.
- **The Metropole Hotel:** a historic treasure that combines traditional and contemporary charm.

Bed & Breakfast: Intimate Hospitality

- **Garnish House:** A Victorian bed and breakfast famed for its friendly staff and excellent meals.
- **Redclyffe Guesthouse:** Cozy and charming, with a personal touch and comfy accommodations.
- **Gabriel House:** This B&B overlooks the city and blends comfort with breathtaking views.

Vacation Rentals: A Home Away from Home

- **Airbnb options:** include anything from metropolitan flats to countryside cottages.
- **Self-Catering Cottages:** With lovely cottages, you may enjoy the freedom of your own space.

- **Waterside Retreats:** Stay near the River Lee for a peaceful respite in the heart of the city.

Dining and Food: A Culinary Journey in Cork

Traditional Irish Pubs: Toasting to Friendship

- **Sin É:** a vibrant pub with traditional Irish music and a welcoming environment.
- **The Oliver Plunkett**: A historic bar with live music and substantial Irish cuisine.
- **An Spailpn Fánach:** A cozy bar with a long history and friendly neighbors.

Culinary Delights: Exploring Cork's Diverse Menu

- **Market Lane:** A popular location with a broad menu that emphasizes local ingredients.
- **Paradiso:** A vegetarian haven noted for its tasty and inventive meals.
- **The Farmgate Café:** Located in the English Market, this restaurant serves fresh, locally sourced cuisine.

Whiskey Distilleries: Tasting Cork's Liquid Gold

- **Jameson Distillery Midleton:** Learn about the history and craftsmanship of Jameson whiskey.
- **The Old Midleton Distillery:** A historic landmark offering tours and premium Irish whiskey samples.
- **Redbreast Distillery:** Known for its single pot still Irish whiskey, this is a must-see for whiskey connoisseurs.

Activities & Sports: Adventure Awaits in Cork

Hiking and Trekking: Discovering the Natural Beauty of Cork

- **Sheeps Head Peninsula:** A beautiful walk with stunning coastline vistas and verdant landscapes.
- **The Ballyhoura Mountains:** a hiker's paradise, with trails for all skill levels.

Water Sports: Riding the Waves and Exploring the Seas

- **Kayaking and Canoeing:** Guided kayaking experiences allow you to explore Cork's waterways.
- **Surfing:** For an exhilarating surfing experience, head to Inchydoney Beach.

- **Sailing:** Explore Cork's coastline with sailing trips and classes for all levels of experience.

Golfing: Teeing off in the Greenery of Cork

- **Top Golf Courses in Cork:** Fota Island Golf Club, Old Head Golf Links, and more.
- **Golf Resorts:** Combine golf with luxurious lodgings for a relaxing getaway.

Cycling Routes: Exploring Cork's Scenic Landscapes

- **The Great Southern Trail:** a scenic bicycle path through beautiful scenery.
- **Beara Peninsula Cycling:** Ride your bike across the rugged beauty of the Beara Peninsula.

Practical Information: Navigating Cork with Ease

Currency and Banking: Managing Your Finances

- **Local currency:** Euro (€)
- **Banking services:** ATMs are generally available, and credit/debit cards are accepted in the majority of institutions.

Emergency Services: Ensuring Safety First

- **Emergency numbers:** 999 and 112 for police, fire, medical assistance, and search and rescue.
- **Medical facilities:** Cork University Hospital (CUH) and local clinics.

Local Customs & Etiquette: Embracing Irish Hospitality

- **Courtesy and friendliness:** The Irish are warm and inviting, and they value courtesy.
- **Respecting Personal space:** Queue patiently and respect personal space in public places.

Language and Communication: Engaging with the Locals

- Although Irish (Gaeilge) is acknowledged, English is the primary language.
- For a cultural touch, learn a few common Irish words.

Health and Safety: Prioritizing Well-being

- No specific vaccinations required, but ensure routine vaccinations are up to date.
- Pharmacies (chemists) widely available for over-the-counter medications.

Conclusion: Reveling in Cork's Tapestry

As we come to the end of our journey through Cork's complex tapestry, I hope this index acts as a compass, leading you through the city's delights. May your tour be filled with amazing experiences, whether you're relishing the flavors of traditional Irish pubs, immersing yourself in Cork's cultural lifeblood, or embarking on outdoor excursions.

Sláinte to Cork, a city that greets visitors with open arms and leaves an unforgettable stamp on their hearts.

Printed in Great Britain
by Amazon

43680180R00086